An Introduc
Using Computers
for Genealogy

THIRD EDITION

David Hawgood

Published by
The Federation of Family History Societies (Publications) Ltd
Units 15-16, Chesham Industrial Centre
Oram Street, Bury, Lancashire BL9 6EN

First published 1994
Second edition 1998
Third edition 2002

ISBN: 1 86006 160 5

Printed and bound by the Alden Group, Oxford and Northamton.

Contents

Preface

This book aims to help anyone with little experience of computers to start using one for family history. The emphasis throughout is on using the computer; you should not have to understand how it works in order to use one.

The first section is about operating a computer. It introduces some of the terminology, and describes the computer keyboard. The second section is about using a computer for correspondence including email, and writing documents. It is a good way to get acquainted with the use of computers. There are descriptions of some of the ways of using a computer with Microsoft Windows programs. There is a common method of operation, so if you learn how to use a Windows word processor it will be much easier for you to use email systems, web browsers, a genealogy package, spreadsheet or database.

Section three describes the use of genealogy packages for recording your personal family history, and printing a variety of family trees and other charts. When you start using a computer, obtain a genealogy package early on. Enter your immediate family and recent ancestors, print some charts. Enter sources of information as you go. It is more important to get experience of use of a genealogy package and a computer than to spend a long time comparing the facilities of packages.

The fourth section is on using computers for family history research. What is useful here is any program that can produce a list, select from it and sort it. This type of facility is available in database packages, word processors, spreadsheets and genealogy packages. Initially, use the one with which you are most familiar. This section also introduces the use of the Internet and data on CDROM disks for family research.

The final section gives a bibliography and describes other sources of help and information. Genealogy is a co-operative hobby; your local family history society is very likely to have some members willing to describe their own use of computers and help you to start using a computer yourself.

The World Wide Web and email have become much the best way of obtaining information about suppliers' and societies' products, indexes, books and addresses. Even if you don't intend to use a computer for processing your own family history information it is worth learning how to use World Wide Web browsers and search engines. It is also worth establishing a web-based email address for yourself so that you can use email from public libraries and Internet cafés. The method is described in Section 2.

World wide web addresses: A full web address starts with http://, for example http://www.hawgood.co.uk. In most browsers anything starting "www" is treated as a web address, the "http://" is supplied. In this book any web address starting www is given without the http:// and is enclosed in angle brackets, e.g. <www.hawgood.co.uk>.

David Hawgood

Using a Computer

Computers and programs

A computer is a machine for processing information. We can **enter** information by typing, **store** it in the computer, **edit** the information in the computer by re-typing only the words or letters that need changing, and **print** all or selected parts. Once the information is in, we can make a **copy** for **transfer** to another computer.

The machinery or **hardware** to do this includes a **keyboard**, a **display screen** and a **printer**. The actual computer part that does the storage and manipulation may only be apparent as slots for insertion of a removable **floppy disk** or **Compact Disk (CD)** used for transfer of information. Transfers may also be made by **communication** along connecting wires, including telephone cables, and by wireless.

A computer has some **programs** stored within it, sets of instructions that tell the computer how to manipulate the information, how to react to the keys we press, what to display on the screen, what to print. Some programs control the computer; they form the **operating system**. Others perform the meaningful manipulation of information; these are **application programs**. **Word processor** programs deal with text. A **spreadsheet** performs calculations on tables of figures. A **database** stores and manipulates lists and tables of information. A **genealogy package** holds information about people and their relationships and prints charts and trees. A **browser** finds and displays information held on remote computers in the **World Wide Web**. **Programs** are known as **software**. A **package** is just a set of programs sold together. Distinctions between the types of application package tend to get blurred. A word processor often can handle tables of figures, a spreadsheet can include text. An **integrated package** often named "**Works**" includes the facilities of a word processor, a spreadsheet and a database, moving information from one to the other.

Information processing for genealogy

What will a computer actually do for us? To answer this we look at three areas of what we do in genealogy: recording our own family relationships and other pedigrees, writing letters and a family history, family research to organise unconnected information and establish how it fits with linked families.

Personal Family History

The development of genealogy packages has made it easy to use a computer for keeping records of family relationships. Typically the screen displays a form with areas for the father, mother and children in one family. Type in the names; add marriage details, date and place of birth and death, sources for each piece of information. Go on to other items such as baptism, burial and a general area of notes about the person. Then you can extend the linked family to grand-children, grandparents and on to other relatives — or you can add unlinked people and link them to the family structure later. For all these people you can rework the information. One good way is to put in outline information first, then go back to the original source documents and progressively enter more detail about people, always with references to the sources. At any stage you can print charts or narrative for one person, a family, ancestors or descendants; ideal for answering letters from other family historians. You can do all this with a genealogy package which you buy, ready to use. These packages are generally inexpensive and of high quality.

Once you have typed in the information you can transfer it to another computer, either in its original form for use by someone else with the same genealogy package, or by putting it into a standard format called GEDCOM which is understood by most genealogy packages.

Email, letters, and other writing

What the computer does sounds simple. You type text, the computer stores it, you can recall it to the screen and edit the text, the computer prints it. The immediate advantages compared with typing are that the text is stored, so you can re-use part or all later; that you can make changes without re-typing a whole page; and that you can print the text with your choice of format, changing the margins and line spacing and typefaces used. The application package you use for this is the **word processor**.

8

These are general purpose programs as used in business and education. There have been enormous efforts by suppliers to make them easier to use. Also the range of facilities included has been extended to handle tables of figures, to handle diagrams and pictures, to put text into columns, to check spelling, to construct an index and many more.

Much of the correspondence for family history now goes by email, prepared in an email program. This looks after the electronic email addresses, and makes it easy to reply to an incoming message, or to send a message to several people at the same time.

In family history we do a lot of writing, both for correspondence and for writing up the results of our research. Word processing and email help us in this. It is very satisfying to send a message and receive a helpful reply within hours, even more satisfying to publish a family history. But another aspect is that so many people use word processing and email at work or college that there is a fair chance you can get help from family and friends. This makes them a relatively easy way in to the mystifying world of computers.

Family research

Both in adding to our knowledge of relatives and in extending our pedigrees, we soon get involved in making lists of people and events, sorting them out to decide which are relevant. The most flexible type of program for this is the general purpose **database** package. These are probably the hardest to use of the types of program mentioned in this book. A genealogy package displays a pre-set form with spaces for names, dates, places and sources. But when using a general purpose database you have to decide which pieces of information to store, allocate names to them, maybe decide the maximum length for each one, and decide whether to store it as text, a date, or a number. As with word processors there are great efforts by suppliers to make databases easier to use, and reduce the amount of computer knowledge needed to get started.

For most purposes for your own family history research you can use a genealogy package, spreadsheet, or word processor. Select one you use already, to save you the effort of learning about a different computer program.

If you will be processing tens of thousands of names for a **one name study** or a **transcription and indexing project**, you are likely to require

9

the facilities of a general purpose database. Use of computers is becoming the common method of undertaking any new indexing projects in family history. The main work and skill is in reading the original hand-written record, typing and checking. The computer can do the work of sorting, indexing and printing, avoiding the necessity of retyping. Many projects are co-operative, with a number of people using the same program for entry of information. In this case participation in a project becomes a good way to gain experience of computing; there will be other people you can ask for help when starting.

The most useful and simplest facilities in processing lists are sorting the items into different orders, selecting them by various criteria and choosing which columns to print and how wide they will be. There are many more complex facilities, such as calculating birth year from age at death, expanding an abbreviated county code to the full name, checking that a code is within an existing list.

There is a great deal of information already held on computers in such a way that you can transfer relevant parts into your own computer. Examples are the **IGI** (International Genealogical Index) **VRI** (Vital Records Index) **Ancestral File** and UK 1881 census from the Church of Jesus Christ of Latter-day Saints; the 1901 UK census from the Public Record Office; indexes to Scottish birth, marriages and deaths from Origins.net; the **National Burial Index** from the Federation of Family History Societies. Some are on the Internet, some on CD, some on both. You can transfer information from them into a genealogy package or into a general purpose database.

Which computer for genealogy?
Many types of computer are adequate for genealogy, with a few genealogy packages available. But the obvious choice is a Personal Computer (PC) with Microsoft Windows operating system. There is a great variety of genealogy programs available. Of genealogists who use computers, over 90% use Windows, so you are more likely to get help.

The Apple Macintosh has excellent facilities, some good genealogy packages and a reputation for being easy to use. Its price is now similar to that of a PC, but because it has been much more expensive in the past there are fewer users in genealogy.

The terminology and details in the rest of the book assume the use of a personal computer (PC) with Windows.

Computer Equipment

Sit down to operate a computer. What do you see? A **keyboard** — the same basic layout as a typewriter but some extra keys. A **mouse** probably — a hand control with buttons; roll it around the table and a pointer moves on the computer screen. The **display screen** — like a television set, or flat like a large calculator. A **printer** — great variety here. Often a **scanner** to transfer text or pictures from paper. The actual computer controls and connects all these and contains information storage devices; it may be a separate box called the **system unit**, it may all be hidden inside the other units. One of the cables at the back may connect this computer to others, in the next room or another continent, generally via the Internet.

The display

After a set time the screen may be blanked or changed to some slowly moving pattern by a screen saver or energy saver, which is disconcerting if you do not expect it; move the mouse or press a key to re-instate the display. Usually the display has a power switch, brightness and contrast controls; they may be hidden at the edge of the screen.

As well as any text or pictures displayed on the screen, three positions may be marked. One is the **cursor**, usually a vertical line or flashing underline showing the current typing position. Press a letter key, that letter appears at the cursor. A second is a **highlight**, a change of brightness or colour on a selected area. The third is the **pointer**, an arrow head on the screen, moved by the mouse. The way these are used depends on the particular program in use. An example is to move the pointer to a box of text, hold down a button on the mouse and 'drag' the box to 'drop' it at a different place on the page when you release the button. You can also move the highlight and pointers around with the arrow keys on the keyboard. On many programs you will find areas of the screen marked as buttons — move the pointer to a displayed "button" and click a real button on the mouse to start an action. Start with one click of the left hand button on the mouse — you might need a double click, and the right button may give different actions.

11

The keyboard

A keyboard layout is shown in Figure 1. One section is much the same as a typewriter with a few extra keys. There are three other groups of keys: Cursor movement keys, the numeric block laid out like a calculator, and function keys. The 102-key layout in the figure is most common on desktop computers. Portable computers often have an 84-key layout; the cursor movement and numeric block are combined and usually the function keys are at one side. Positions of some of the special and symbol keys may vary. Do read the manual for your computer and your programs about the use of the keyboard; there are variations.

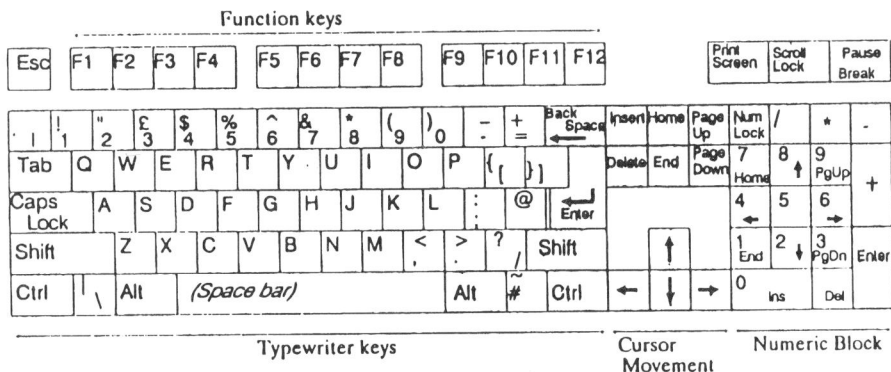

Figure 1. Keyboard layout on a Personal Computer for Windows.

Note that the keyboard is under control of a program. Any key can be made to perform any function specified by the programmer. Pressing letter F may mean the usual 'add a letter F to the text at the cursor' or in a genealogy package it may mean 'show details of the Father of the current person', or it may mean anything else. Note also that if you hold a key down, after a pause its action is repeated rapidly. The pause and rate of repeat can be set to suit you.

Keys to press with another

On a typewriter you press a shift key together with a letter key to get a capital letter. On a computer there are other similar keys, **Ctrl** meaning 'Control' and **Alt** meaning 'Alternate'. If a manual tells you to 'Press Alt and H to get Help' you press **Alt**, hold it down, then press and release H. The Alt key on the right (sometimes marked **Alt Gr**) usually acts the same

12

as **Alt** but it can give a third character from a key, a facility mainly used on keyboards for languages with accented letters. When using a mouse, the Shift, Control and Alt keys also change the meaning of mouse operations.

Mode switch (toggle) keys

On a typewriter there is a 'Caps lock' key. Press it down, all letters are in capitals until you press 'Caps lock' again. A computer has a **Caps Lock** key, similar except that it only affects letters but not numbers and symbols. In computer jargon this type of key is called a **toggle**, like an electrical toggle switch which stays on or off. Another toggle is **Insert**. This changes from insert mode, where pressing a letter key inserts it at the cursor, to typeover mode, where pressing a letter key replaces the one at the cursor. **Num Lock** changes the operation of the whole group of keys laid out like a calculator to provide cursor movement instead (and **Shift** changes this operation just while it is held down).

Keys which do something

The letters, numbers and symbols are much the same as on a typewriter, but there are more symbols. **Delete** removes the character at the cursor, **Backspace** removes the character before the cursor. The **Enter** key has two uses: it is the equivalent of the carriage return on the typewriter, it also terminates and acts on a typed command. **Tab** moves to the next tab stop when typing text; it is also used to move on from one area of a form to the next, e.g. from birth date to birth place. To move backwards, i.e. **back-tab**, press Shift and Tab together. Function keys F1 to F12 have meanings entirely dependent on the program in use, though F1 is usually reserved for summoning help. **Print Screen** with Windows puts a copy of the screen contents (including graphics) in a temporary storage space called the **clip-board**. The simplest way to print it is to start a Windows word processor, choose **paste** which puts the clip-board contents into a document, and print the document.

We are left with cursor movement keys. Up, down, left and right arrows move one line or character; with **Control** they move further. **Home** and **End** typically move to the start or finish of a line or document or list. **Page Up** and **Page Down** move to the previous or next page. There are many variations on the use of these keys and combinations with others.

Pause, Break, Stop, Escape, Undo

If you press a key and the facility shown is not what you wanted, the Escape key (marked Esc) will often take you back a stage. If the program has already made a change, look for **Undo** which is often on the Edit menu.

If you want to halt a program, look first on the screen for a displayed button marked "stop" or "cancel" or "abort", and click the mouse on it. Even if you have a key on the keyboard marked **Pause** and **Break** it will probably have no effect. Next, try to exit from the program. Exit or Quit from a program are often on the file menu, so if the program seems to be working but you cannot see a way out, try pressing Alt with function key F4, or Alt with letter F. In extremis if nothing else works, press Control and Alt and Delete, all three together. Beware — this may re-start (re-boot) the computer. But on Windows systems you will probably get a message first, which may tell you whether the program is stuck, and what options you have for stopping or re-starting. Always exit from all programs correctly if at all possible; if you just turn off or re-boot the computer you may lose some information. If you cannot see a "stop" button, try looking on the "start" menu.

Accented letters and special symbols

About 95 different characters are marked on the keyboard, taking upper and lower case letters, digits and symbols. The characters have numbered codes; those on the keyboard are mainly codes 32 to 127, for example in the ASCII character set capital A is code 65. More codes are available for other characters, including accented letters. These can be obtained from the keyboard but to do this you have to find the code, from tables in your operating system or word processor manuals To include one in text, hold down the Alt key and type the number, using the number keys in the numeric block, not those above the letters. For example to type an e acute (é) hold down Alt, type 130, then release Alt. But an easier way in Windows is to use an accessory program called Character Map. In some programs this is available from an Insert menu as "Insert Character". In others it has to be started separately (Click Start, point to Programs, point to Accessories, point to System Tools, and click Character Map.) As there are different character sets in use, these characters sometimes come out differently when transferred to another program, or even when printed. Not all programs accept characters with numbers over 127.

14

The mouse

The mouse complements the keyboard in the control of the computer. The mouse gets its name from the long thin tail which connects it to the computer. Move the mouse on the table, a pointer moves on the screen. If you need precise control it is easier if you rest your wrist on the table. You can pick up the mouse and move it to a convenient place on the table without moving the pointer. Usually there are two buttons on the mouse. Most operations require one click of the left hand button, some require two clicks in quick succession; you can set the time interval. The right button gives different actions, for example display of a small menu of available facilities. On portable computers there is an equivalent device such as a tracker ball.

Printer

The main types of printer on the market are dot matrix, laser and ink jet. Laser printers give excellent quality, have the highest initial price (particularly for colour printing) and reasonable running costs. Ink jet print quality is almost as good, the initial cost is lower (particularly for colour, and large sheets of paper), the running cost is higher. Dot matrix quality is lower, but still very good in 'near letter quality' (NLQ); running cost is lower, and you can print on continuous stationery whereas the others use cut sheets of paper.

Information Storage

The measure of information storage space is the **byte**. A kilobyte (or K, Kb) is 1024 bytes — computers work in binary numbers, so 1024 (which is 2 to the power of 10) is a more convenient number than 1000. Similarly a megabyte (or M, Mb) is 1024 x 1024 bytes, which is 1,048,576, and a Gigabyte is 1024 x 1024 x 1024, about 1074 million bytes. The code for one character, for example one letter, occupies one byte. Because there is considerable repetition in text or pictures, information can be compressed; a typical result is that the effective space available is doubled.

Storage devices

The computer has some Random Access Memory (RAM) as semi-conductor chips inside. It has some Read Only Memory (ROM) — as a minimum a **bootstrap** program, which loads or 'boots' other parts of the operating system from disk — the computer 'pulls itself up by its own bootstrap'. It will also have some built in storage, probably using magnetic recording on a **hard disk**, and some removable and exchangeable storage, probably a magnetic floppy disk and a CD drive for optical reading of disks similar to music compact disks. But the built in storage could all be semi-conductor chips, particularly in a portable computer. The removable storage may be in semi-conductor chips on a plug-in device like a credit card, or it may be magnetic tape, mainly used as **back-up** (security copies of the non-removable storage). CD drives may be read-only or may provide writing as well; DVD (Digital Versatile Disk) drives also read CDs.

Whichever it is, the computer considers a storage device as a 'drive' and allocates a letter (with a colon). Usually the first floppy disk drive is 'A:', the second floppy (if fitted) is 'B:', part or all of the hard disk is 'C:', the CD-ROM is 'D:'. Other parts of the hard disk and extra devices have other letters. When the computer is turned on it generally loads by looking at drive A for a disk; if there is no disk it looks at drive C.

Diskettes or **floppy disks**: the main type of exchangeable floppy disk is a 3½" disk in a rigid plastic case, a "high density" disk holding 1.44 megabytes. The disk has to be formatted before use by recording a magnetic pattern of concentric circles; the operating system has a command to format disks. The recorded information can be protected so no other information can be recorded (written). To **write protect**, move a slider to open a hole in one corner.

There are other types of diskette in use. Mainly superseded is the 5¼" floppy disk in a square cardboard envelope. There are various exchangeable disks with much higher capacity, 100 Megabytes to several Gigabytes on a disk.

Files

A file is a collection of related information. It can be recorded and given a name, just as you write a name on a document wallet or box of papers. A computer file may contain a word processor document, a genealogy database, or a program. Operations to move or copy the file are independent of its contents. A file has a name with two parts. The first part is the actual name; it is best to stick to letters and digits, though some symbols are permitted. The second part, after a full stop, is the **extension**, which shows the category of file. Some extensions are recognised by the operating system, for example .EXE is a program, .TXT is text without word processor formatting controls. Others are particular to an application package; .FTW for a genealogy database for the program *Family Tree Maker for Windows*. On some systems filenames are restricted to eight characters.

Directories or Folders
The operating system places a file on a drive where there is room; it keeps a record of file location against file name; this list also has the date and time the file was last changed. For convenience one drive can have several different directories or folders, given names like file names. This makes it appear that a drive contains directories and files; a directory in its turn can contain other directories (sub-directories) and files. The **path** to specify a file has the drive letter (with a colon), then a succession of directory and sub-directory names, then the file name. The parts are separated by backslash characters, for example d:\wp\ffhs\ch1.wp.

Figure 2 shows directory or folder structure (on the left) and contents of one folder (on the right); it is a display from Windows Explorer. It shows a folder "Nbi" which I used while testing the National Burial Index on CDROM. On the left, it shows that drive C contains a folder "Program

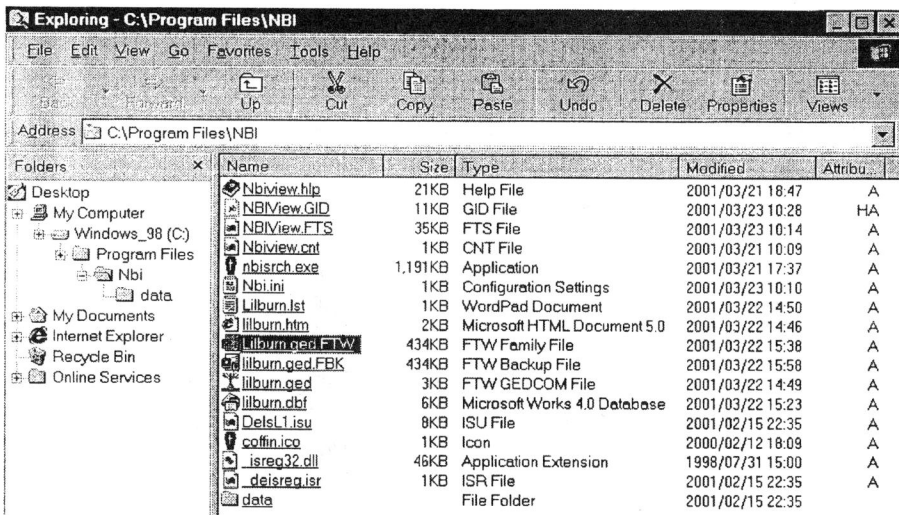

Name	Size	Type	Modified	Attribu..
Nbiview.hlp	21KB	Help File	2001/03/21 18:47	A
NBIView.GID	11KB	GID File	2001/03/23 10:28	HA
NBIView.FTS	35KB	FTS File	2001/03/23 10:14	A
Nbiview.cnt	1KB	CNT File	2001/03/21 10:09	A
nbisrch.exe	1,191KB	Application	2001/03/21 17:37	A
Nbi.ini	1KB	Configuration Settings	2001/03/23 10:10	A
Lilburn.lst	1KB	WordPad Document	2001/03/22 14:50	A
lilburn.htm	2KB	Microsoft HTML Document 5.0	2001/03/22 14:46	A
Lilburn.ged.FTW	434KB	FTW Family File	2001/03/22 15:38	A
lilburn.ged.FBK	434KB	FTW Backup File	2001/03/22 15:58	A
lilburn.ged	3KB	FTW GEDCOM File	2001/03/22 14:49	A
lilburn.dbf	6KB	Microsoft Works 4.0 Database	2001/03/22 15:23	A
DelsL1.isu	8KB	ISU File	2001/02/15 22:35	A
coffin.ico	1KB	Icon	2000/02/12 18:09	A
_isreg32.dll	46KB	Application Extension	1998/07/31 15:00	A
_deisreg.isr	1KB	ISR File	2001/02/15 22:35	A
data		File Folder	2001/02/15 22:35	

Figure 2. Folders (Directories) and Files in Windows Explorer

17

Files". This is standard in Windows systems, and when you install any new program it is likely to suggest putting it here. Accordingly, when I loaded the NBI disc I followed the suggested procedure, which gave me this folder "Nbi" in the Program Files. The hierarchy continues down to a folder "data" within "Nbi". Looking at the files in "Nbi", the first six whose names start "Nbi" came with the program. "nbisrch.exe" is the actual program, the others are small files which it uses. The next group starting "Lilburn" are ones I generated while testing. I created a GEDCOM file lilburn.ged and imported it into Family Tree Maker, giving a database Lilburn.ged.ftw. There were some error reports while the file was processed, these were put into a file lilburn.lst which is a text file which can be read by Wordpad — which comes with Windows. While testing I also created a web page which is lilburn.htm, and a database which is lilburn.dbf. Note that the column headed "type"shows what program I have set to process files with a particular extension — here the GEDCOM file is set to be processed by Family Tree Maker, it could be processed by another genealogy package, or I could set it to be viewed by Wordpad if I wanted to look at the contents of the GEDCOM file rather than having it processed. The files as shown are in reverse order of names, which happened to suit my purpose. I could have sorted the files another way, e.g. into date order.

Driving a Computer

Almost all operation of computers including Internet browsing now starts from a **Graphical User Interface** or **GUI**. The essence of this is that the screen displays lists and menus of possible actions, small pictures ("icons") representing them, a form to fill in, or text with underlined and coloured action words. To choose any of these, move the pointer to the appropriate place on the screen using the mouse or keyboard arrows, then click the mouse or press the Enter key. Depending on the operation you may now need to drag holding down a mouse button, or type text. The details of operation are different with different computers and operating systems, but the overall style of operation is similar. It is known as "WIMP" or Windows, Icons, Mouse, Pointer operation. The "windows" are independent areas of the screen, such that information from several programs can be displayed at the same time. It is also possible to have several programs running, each occupying the full screen, and switch between them. What follows gives examples of control using icons, file lists, and Internet browsers. One general tip is to make a note of the steps needed to start programs on your own computer.

File list

In this method of control, the display is a list of names of programs, maybe with names of documents and other files. One name is picked out by a highlight. Use the arrow keys on the keyboard, or the mouse, to move the highlight to the one you want. To start the program press the Enter key, or click the mouse button . You will normally get a choice of displaying these as a hierarchy, like the left hand side of Figure 2, or as a list, the right hand side of Figure 2. For example, clicking on nbisrch.exe is one way to start the National Burial Index program. Windows tries to do something appropriate if you click on any file name. For example clicking on the family database Lilburn.ged.ftw starts Family Tree Maker and displays the Lilburn records which I extracted from the NBI.

Icons

Figure 3 shows icons. For example there is a picture of a coffin for the National Burial Index program. Use the mouse to move the pointer to the picture of the coffin, click the mouse button, the NBI program starts.

Figure 3. Icons in Windows.

19

Michael Cass was married to Mary Spavin on 2 Oct 1813 in St Leonard, New Malton, Yorks [4]. **Mary Spavin** was born in 1795/96 in Ryton, Yorks [3]. She was in the census in 1851 in 1 Middlebrook Court, Bailgate, Lincoln [8]. Michael Cass and Mary Spavin had the following children:

- +3 i. <u>**Thomas Cass**</u>.
- +4 ii. <u>**William Cass**</u>.
- +5 iii. <u>**Sarah Cass**</u>.
- 6 iv. **Jane Cass** was christened on 20 Dec 1820 in Saint Mary and Saint Nicholas, Beverley, Yorks [4].
- 7 v. **Elizabeth Cass** was christened on 5 Apr 1827 in St Mary Magdalene, Lincoln [9].

Figure 4. Text with links, hypertext, as used in Internet browsers.

Browsers, Hypertext and HTML

A method of operation used in Help systems and Internet browsing is becoming more common in general operation of computers. The essence of it is that the text on the display screen has some words or phrases marked, usually by underlining and colouring. Each has a link address or **Uniform Resource Locator** (URL), not visible on the screen. Click on the underlined section, the system fetches and displays the page from that link address — which may be in your own computer, or may be a Web page accessed remotely via the Internet. This text incorporating links is known as **Hypertext**, it is generated using **HTML** which is **HyperText Markup Language**, and can be viewed using an Internet **browser**. Figure 4 shows some details of the family of Michael Cass, with hypertext links. Clicking the mouse on the underlined names of Thomas, William or Sarah Cass displays pages showing details of their families. There is no extra information for Jane or Elizabeth Cass, so these names are not underlined. Clicking on the underlined footnote numbers displays pages giving the text of the footnotes, which are the source references for the family information. This particular page was generated initially on my own computer by the genealogy package Family Origins; I later copied it onto an Internet Web site, so anyone could obtain these family details.

Command Line

Before Graphic User Interfaces were in general use, control was by typing in commands to tell the computer what to do. For example with **MSDOS** the Microsoft Disk Operating System, typing "DIR" lists the files in a directory. Because the system prompts the user for the next command on completion of a task, the interface is known as the **DOS Prompt**. You may encounter parts of the command structure within a graphical interface, for example **wildcard** characters ★ (asterisk) meaning "any set of characters", ? (query) meaning "any one character". You may also encounter command operation with some Internet operations, for example when transferring a file to or from a Web site.

Typing Documents, Letters and Email Messages

Most family historians with computers use them for typing documents some of the time, and most use email. We write away for information and write up our notes. Typing a document into a computer is much the same as using a typewriter. The main differences are:

- What you type appears on the screen first, not on the paper
- You can go back to what you have typed and make changes
- You can print part or all of the document at any stage
- You can keep the document in the computer, to use again later
- You can change the format of the document without having to type it again

In a reply to an email, you can copy part of the incoming message, and you don't have to re-type the email addresses.

Word processing is the use of a computer for typing documents and performing a variety of associated functions. A **word processing package** is a set of computer programs; it may also be just called a **word processor**, though that term is also used for a computer together with a word processing package.

Word processing is a good way to start using a computer:

- Compared with other ways of using computers, it is more like ordinary life and involves less computer jargon.
- Many people use word processors, so you are more likely to be able to get help on this than on other ways of using computers.
- You get into the way of finding and storing files on the computer without having to consider how they are organised. Usually there is just one file for each document, and you choose its name. The file management will use the facilities of the operating system, but tailored to use with word processing, so you can use it to find, store and copy documents.

- There are more introductory books and training on word processing than on any other use of computers.
- It is very useful in family history research. As well as writing letters you can write research plans, summaries, transcripts, lists of sources searched, articles, news-letters. You can incorporate reports from genealogy packages, general purpose databases or spreadsheets, modifying them in the word processor.

Typing a letter using the computer

Typing a letter is a familiar operation. This Section describes how to do it using a computer, to point out some things which are different between using a computer and using a typewriter. The aim is to introduce computer methods in the context of the familiar task.

As an example, figure 5 shows a letter written after we visited the grave of my wife's Aunt Lorna in Australia. Here are the steps needed to produce it, using the word processor *Wordpad* which is part of Microsoft Windows 98.

The processes needed to start a program, choose a menu or select an area of text become second nature when you have used Windows for a little time. The operation of all Windows programs is similar.

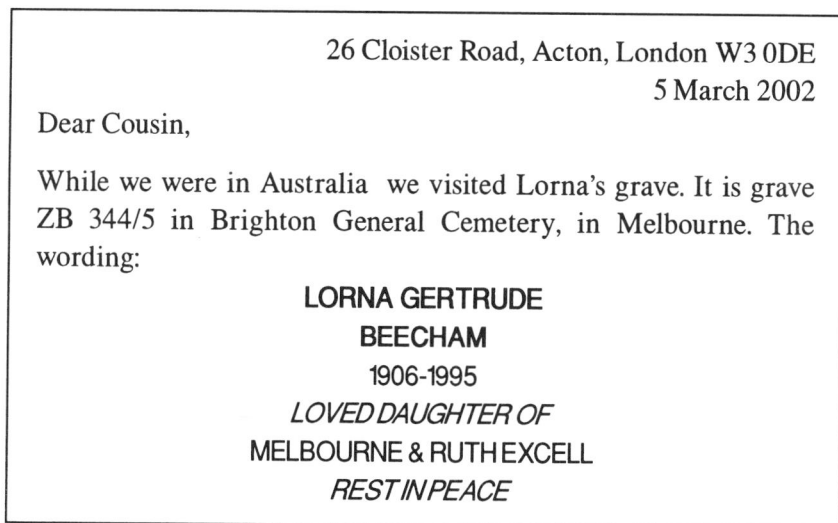

---

26 Cloister Road, Acton, London W3 0DE
5 March 2002

Dear Cousin,

While we were in Australia we visited Lorna's grave. It is grave ZB 344/5 in Brighton General Cemetery, in Melbourne. The wording:

LORNA GERTRUDE

BEECHAM

1906-1995

LOVED DAUGHTER OF

MELBOURNE & RUTH EXCELL

REST IN PEACE

Figure 5. A letter typed using Windows *Wordpad* word processor.

In Windows 98 there are several alternative ways of starting programs — from the start menu list of programs, from Explorer, from "My Computer", and probably most used by having a "short cut" as an icon on the starting screen or "desktop". You can set up these "short cut" icons to suit your preferences, and move them around on the "desktop" screen. When I prepared this example I used Windows 98, and started *Wordpad* from an icon on the Desktop screen.

Start the word processor. A typing screen opens up, with a menu along the top (File, Edit, View, Insert, Format, Help). I want a ruler visible, to show tabs and margins, and also a format bar for easy changes of font (typeface), and paragraph alignment. Click on the "View" menu and choose "Ruler". I also wanted the Format Bar visible — in Figure 6 this is the line starting with "Times New Roman", the name of a font. What are the other items on the format bar? One way to find out is to use the mouse to move the pointer slowly along the line — a brief description appears against each item. The last but one is "Align Right", so I clicked on this because I want the first line with my address to end on the right margin. A brief description of the facility also appears in the status bar at the bottom of the window — here "Right-justifies paragraph".

An alternative way to set right alignment is to choose "Paragraph" from the Format menu, as shown in Figure 7. You might expect to be able to set the page margins as well from here, but it seems to be missing. How to find it? Use the "Help" facility. Click "Help", then "Help topics", choose "Search", type "margins". One of three topics displayed is "To set page margins", display this and you are told to click "Page Setup" on the File menu. Facilities are not always where you think they should be — use "Help" to find them.

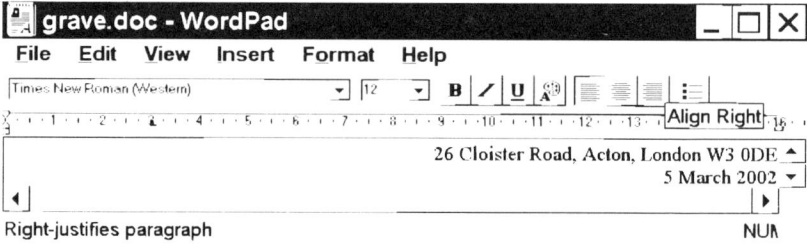

Figure 6. Ruler, Toolbar, and Status Bar.

24

| File | Edit | View | Insert | Format | Help |

Times New Roman (Western)

Font...

Bullet Style

· · 1 · · 2 · · 3 · · 4 · · 5 · ·

Paragraph...

Dear Cousin,

While we were **Tabs...**

in Brighton General Cemetery, in Melbourne. The wording:

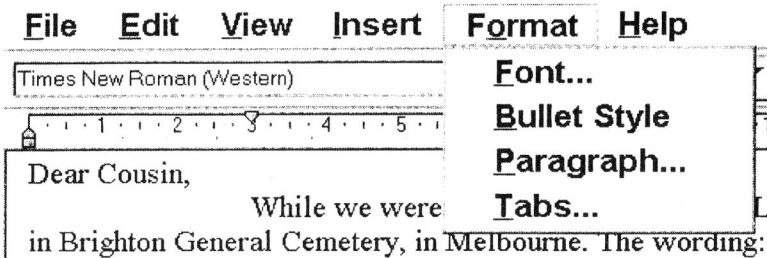

Figure 7. Drop-down menu.

After putting in the date on the right, and salutation on the left, I wanted an indent for the next line. I found two ways to do this. For one, I clicked on the ruler to make a tab stop where I wanted the indent, then just pressed the tab key before typing the paragraph. The aim in Windows and other systems with a graphical user interface is to make the operation as similar as possible to a manual system. The other way was to use "Paragraph" on the "Format" menu; from here I could choose Left and Right indentation for the whole paragraph, and the first line indentation I wanted.

The font for the first few lines of the letter is Times Roman, designed for easy reading in newspapers and books. After I typed the wording of the memorial inscription, I decided to make it look similar to the actual gravestone. I tried several including "Trajan" derived from Roman inscriptions, but the one nearest was Arial, commonly used on computer screens. To select text to change its appearance, move the pointer to the start of the piece of text, depress the mouse button, move the pointer to the end of the text of interest, release. The selected text is highlighted, as white on black; once text is selected it can be deleted, moved, or changed in various ways. First I selected the text of the whole inscription, and changed the font directly from the format bar – clicking on the down arrow after the font name gave a list of all available fonts, I clicked on the one I wanted. To change the last line to italic, I selected just that line, and clicked the *I* in the format bar. I could have made both these changes using the format menu, as shown in Figure 8, but the format bar gives access to the most commonly used facilities. Most applications have a choice of several tool bars, status bars, etc. They tend to be most useful once you have become accustomed to the facilities available.

Font ? X

Font:	Font style:	Size:	
Arial	Bold	12	OK

Font:
Arial

- 𝕋𝕋 AmerType Md BT
- 𝕋𝕋 Animals 1
- 𝕋𝕋 Animals 2
- Arial
- 𝕋𝕋 Arial Black
- 𝕋𝕋 Arial Narrow
- 𝕋𝕋 AvantGarde Bk BT

Font style:
Bold

- Regular
- Italic
- Bold
- Bold Italic

Size:
12

- 12
- 14
- 16
- 18
- 20
- 22
- 24

OK

Cancel

Effects

☐ Strikeout

☐ Underline

Color:
Black

Sample

AaBbYyZz

Script:
Western

This is a TrueType font. This same font will be used on both your printer and your screen.

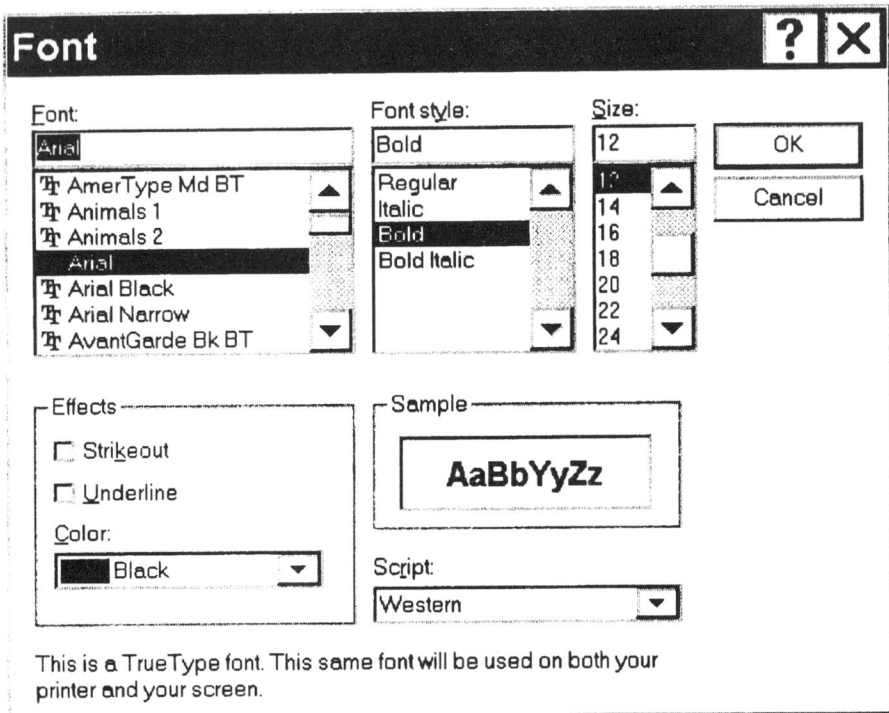

Figure 8. Changing a font.

To save the file, select the File menu and choose 'Save as', then type a file name in the appropriate box. If it is a letter you want to keep, make sure you make a back-up copy on a removable medium such as a floppy disk, zip disk or writable CD as well as the main copy on the hard disk. In all your computing, it is very important to make systematic copies of files onto removable media. The end of the day, or maybe the end of the week, is a good time to make systematic back-up copies.

The final step is to print the letter. This facility is available on the File menu. Because there is one print manager which applies to all Windows programs, printing is usually easy.

Email from a web page

When you start using computers, or thinking about buying one, subscribe to a web-based email service. Most of them are free, financed by

Welcome davidhawgood@mail.com
You are using 0% of your mail quota.

my mail *account*

📧 **You have new mail** 🎵 Write Message ✉ Personal Folders

🔊 **Write Message** 📁 Personal Folders 📧 Mail.com Promotions

📞 PC2Phone Calls ⚡ Premium Services

mail.com *services*

Special Introductory Rate
of $9.99 - normally $19.95!!!

cool *offers*

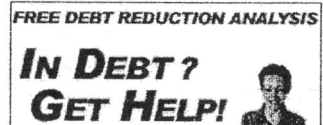

Figure 9. Main screen of web-based email from www.mail.com

advertisements. The advantage is that you can use the service on any computer with Internet access — at a public library, in a cyber café, etc. You can look for new messages, reply to them, write messages and store your old messages so that you can access them again from any computer. The best known is Hotmail, but it does have the disadvantage that mail disappears after 45 days if not accessed. There are others which keep mail much longer. I use <www.mail.com>. This gives a choice of a number of types of address. They can end in mail.com, post.com, london.com, teacher.com and other places and occupations.

To open a new account, access <www.mail.com>, e.g. by "Start" and "Run" in Windows. When the service connects choose "New Member Sign Up" on the screen. Choose an email address, for example I have davidhawgood@mail.com. Choose a password, fill in a form with your home address, date of birth and sex. Immediately it is possible to send and receive emails — the basic screen is in Figure 9.

To start a new message, choose "write message", type an email address, a subject and the text of the message. One tip here is that you can prepare the text in advance in a word processor, then copy and paste it into the email.

Receiving a message, click on "You have new mail", this shows the list of messages from the in-box. I clicked on "Lilburn ancestors" and received the message shown in Figure 10.

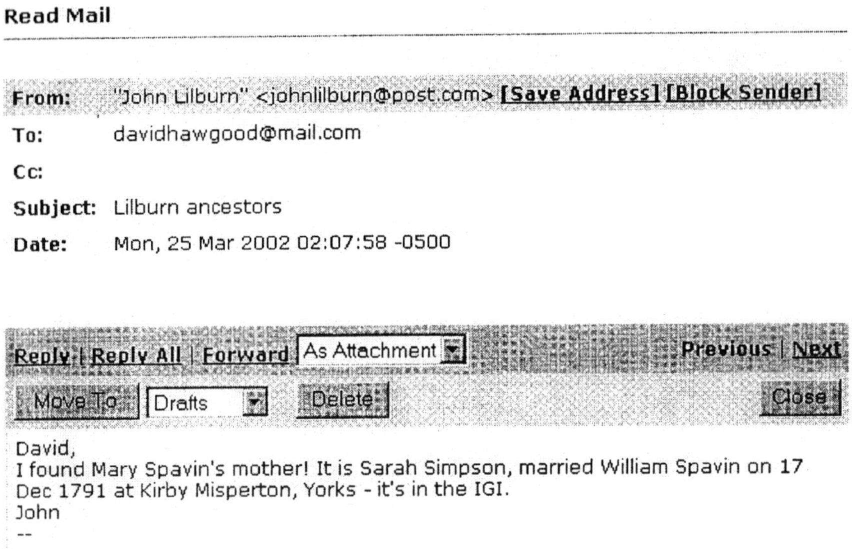

From: "John Lilburn" <johnlilburn@post.com> **[Save Address] [Block Sender]**

To: davidhawgood@mail.com

Cc:

Subject: Lilburn ancestors

Date: Mon, 25 Mar 2002 02:07:58 -0500

Reply | Reply All | Forward | As Attachment ▼ | Previous | Next

Move To | Drafts ▼ | Delete | Close

David,
I found Mary Spavin's mother! It is Sarah Simpson, married William Spavin on 17
Dec 1791 at Kirby Misperton, Yorks - it's in the IGI.
John
--

Figure 10. Receiving an email message.

Facilities for replying to messages and forwarding them make email very convenient. Click "Reply" and the incoming message is copied into a reply with subject and email address already filled in. Do delete the unwanted parts of the message, just keep enough to make it clear what you are replying to. Figure 11 shows this, with a section of the incoming message embedded in the reply.

Note in Figure 11 that you can choose font, colour, paragraph justification, etc, just as in word processing. I recommend that for emails you keep the very simple default format. It can be read by any email system.

Do file your emails in folders with names you choose. When writing this book I went to "Personal folders" on the menu bar as shown in figure 9, and created one called "ffhs book". Figure 12 shows how choosing "Move to" lets one choose drafts, inbox, trash, or any named personal folder. A common mistake by people starting to use email is to leave all the messages in the "in-box" or "Sent" folder. It makes life simpler later on if you file them in folders with meaningful names.

Note that these folders in web-based email are not the folders or directories of the computer you are sitting at — they are folders set up within the email service.

To:	"John Lilburn" <johnlilburn@post.com>

Cc:		BCc:	

Subject: Re: Lilburn ancestors

Paragraph ▼	Font ▼	Size ▼

Text Color ▼	Text Background Color ▼

☐ **View HTML source** | **Clear Format**

✂ 📋 📋 **B** *I* <u>U</u> ≡ ≡ ≡ ≣ ≣ ⅗ ⅗ 🌐

Switch to Basic Editor

John,

you wrote: > I found Mary Spavin's mother! It is Sarah Simpson,
married William Spavin on 17 Dec 1791 at Kirby Misperton,
Yorks - it's in the IGI. <

That's great, I will look at the microfilm,

David.

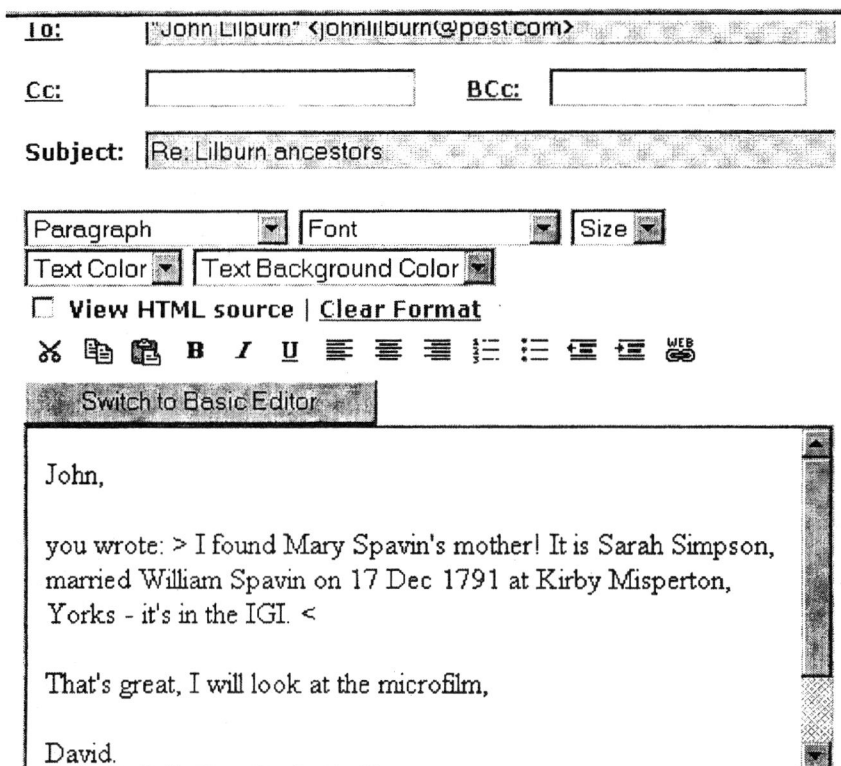

Figure 11. Reply to email.

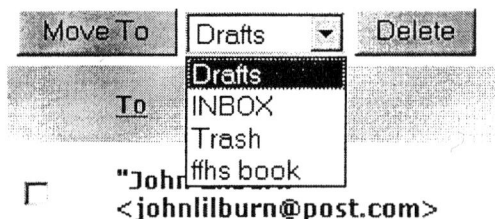

Move To	Drafts ▼	Delete

	Drafts
To	INBOX
	Trash
☐ "John	ffhs book

<johnlilburn@post.com>

Figure 12. Filing an email.

Personal Family History

Genealogy Packages

This section is about using a computer to organise and print information for related people. The method described is the use of computer programs on sale for this purpose: lineage-linked genealogy packages. These programs come ready to use. You copy the program onto your computer, then immediately type information about people and your sources of information. You do not have to decide how the information is to be stored and it does not matter which person you enter first. Then you can print a family tree or chart, choosing which person to start from and which style of chart you want. Later you can add more people.

I have used many different genealogy packages. Each one has increased my knowledge of my family history. Every time I use a package I realise that there are gaps in my knowledge. I work over the information for part of the family, check back to documents, phone or email around the family, and enter the extra information.

Based on my experience, I believe that your knowledge of family history will gain from the use of almost any genealogy package. Use it for the part of the family where you are trying to get the information organised.

At the beginning do not worry too much about the lists of facilities available in particular packages. Go for ease of use, or ease of getting help. But there is one facility which can save you having to retype your information if you change to another genealogy package. This is availability of GEDCOM, a standard for transfer of genealogical data from one computer or package to another.

There are packages available for almost every type of computer — the books and magazines listed in Section 5 will help you find one. Which package is 'best' is a matter of opinion and keeps changing as new programs and new versions appear. There is a note about buying packages at the end of this section, and some addresses of suppliers in Section 5.

Most packages present an outline family structure on the screen. Into this you type your information about names, dates, places, etc, together with a note of your sources. As far as computer knowledge and experience go, if you can use a word processor you should be able to use the preset facilities of a genealogy package to enter family information and print charts. Some have more complex facilities as well, so that you can define different types of information to enter, specify selection criteria, and design the layout of reports. Genealogy packages designed to run with Microsoft Windows use the same standard type of user control as other Windows programs, moving a pointer on the screen with the mouse, clicking it to select a person or an action. Other programs have their own particular controls, mainly selecting by number from menus, or pressing function keys.

Entering information

Different packages have different styles of entry. The example is from Family Origins. Figure 13 shows its family screen, showing the children, their parents and grandparents. You can move a highlight to any person; in the example it is on Michael Cass, father in this family. More details of that person appear in the upper area of the screen. By clicking on arrows you can move to an earlier or later generation. To help this, an arrowhead precedes the name in the column on the left if that person has children. For a person with several spouses, a box "other spouses" appears above their name, and you can choose which one is shown. One item in the toolbar is "Explorer (find a person)" shown as a torch symbol. This gives a list of people in alphabetical order, to help in selecting the family of interest, with facilities to search by the contents of any field.

To change the details of a person, move the highlight to their name and double click, or choose the edit menu then "Individual". The screen changes to that shown in Figure 14, a list of items of information. To add another item choose "Add fact" — this gives a list of about 50 possible facts — from Adoption to Will via Education, Military Service and Retirement. For each you can put in the date, and the place or name. Note that there can be several similar facts, here Michael Cass was shown as a brick-layer when he had a child christened in 1814, and as a mason in 1818. For each you can add a source, and note about the item — against the 1818 occupation of mason I added a note that he was shown as a mason on the

31

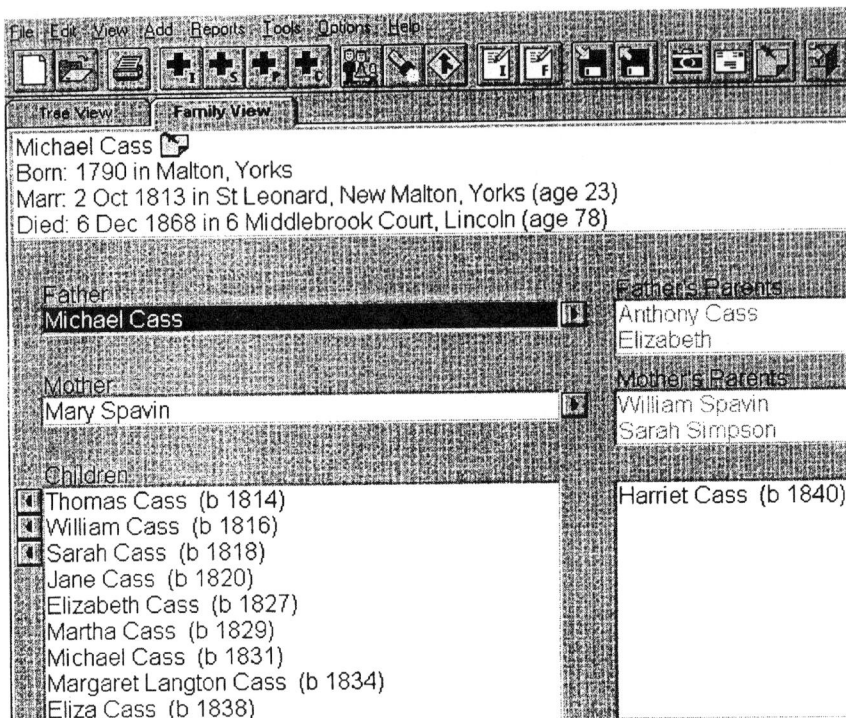

Figure 13. Family screen of Family Origins.

christenings of all subsequent children. Once this is added, an X appears in the column marked "N".

Entering sources

The column marked "S" in Figure 14 shows whether a source has been entered for that fact. I find that using a genealogy package makes me more systematic, particularly in making sure I record what source documents I have used. The way sources can be recorded in genealogy packages has improved over the years. Continuing this example in Family Origins, Figure 15 shows entry of the information about the source document. The short name shows it comes from the parish register of Old Malton in Yorkshire. The full description shows I looked at a transcript, available to me at the Society of Genealogists. It is also possible to enter details of author, publisher, and source text. This document description applies to

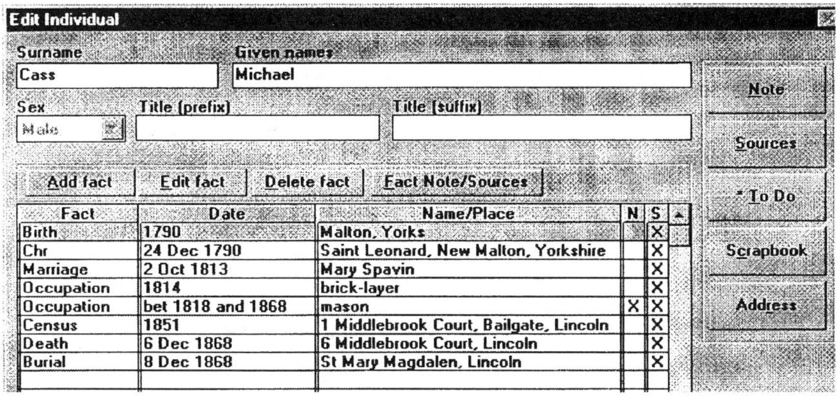

Figure 14. Screen for editing information about a person.

all references found in this transcript — in this case, christenings of several children. Figure 16 shows entry of the citation, against my use of this document as the source for Michael Cass being a bricklayer in 1814 — the entry for the christening of his son Thomas.

Family Origins also adds a "To Do" list, tasks linked to a person record and a repository record. If going to a particular record office, you can print a list of the tasks you have "To Do" there.

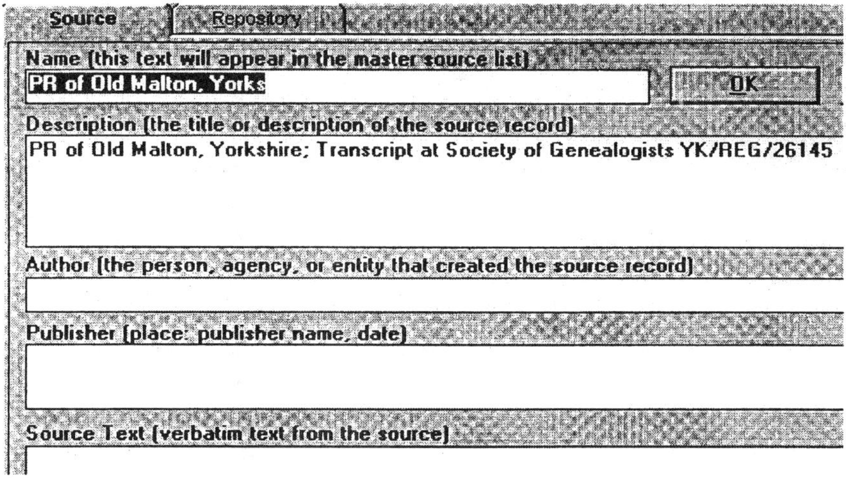

Figure 15. Adding a source.

Source Citation

Source: PR of Old Malton, Yorks

Citation Details (page number, volume, etc)

chr. of Thomas 15 Jul 1814 shows father Michael as bricklayer

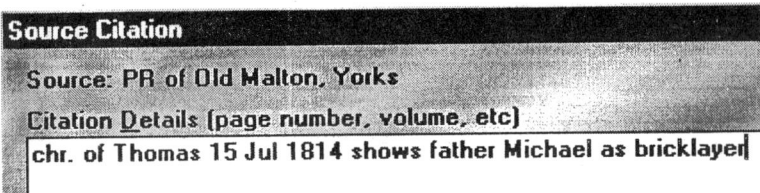

Figure 16. Source citation.

Printing Family Trees and Charts

Once you have entered your family information, genealogy packages have a great variety of ways of displaying or printing it. The styles go from text alone, through text with linking lines, to graphics with fancy boxes and photographs and even pictures of leafy trees. The content may be full information about one person, summary lists of names and dates for many people, a family group sheet showing details for a couple and their children, a chart of descendants of one person, or a birth brief showing the pedigree of ancestors of one person. As well as variants on these, there are charts showing how two people are related, timeline charts showing the lives of people as lines against a scale of years, and others. In this book there are examples of a drop line family tree, an indented descendants chart and an ancestors chart.

Printing a chart is usually a question and answer operation. First choose the type of chart, person from whom it starts, and number of generations. This defines the people to be included and how they are linked. Choose a layout, and which pieces of information to be included. Usually there is a basic (default) layout at the start, so you can just print a preset style without making any decisions except the person to start from. Choose whether to look at the chart on the display screen, print it immediately, or put it into a disk file. If you use the last method, 'print to disk', you can incorporate the chart into a word processor document.

Maybe that all sounds too easy? If there is a problem, it is a familiar one in family history. Once you incorporate the whole family on a tree, it becomes too large to be convenient. Whether you draw the tree by hand on a roll of wall-paper or print a mass of separate pages in the computer and stick them together, the result becomes too big to take on visits to the family or the record office. The answer is to print charts for selected parts of the family. You will also find that some types of chart are attractive as

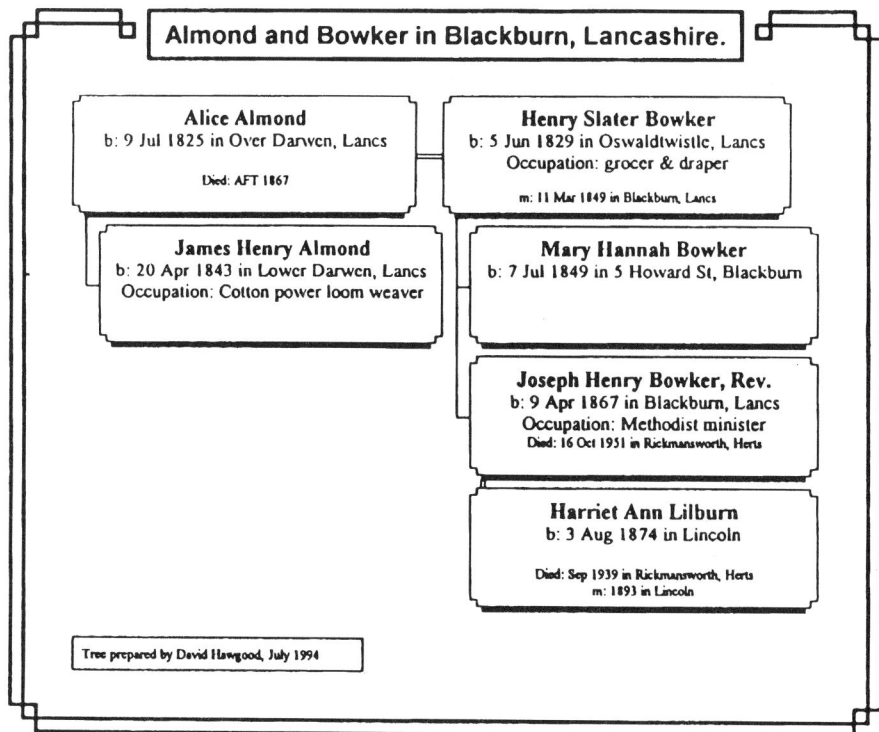

Figure 17. Descendants Tree from Family Tree Maker for Windows.

presents for other members of the family, but other types are convenient to take to the record office because they contain a large amount of information compressed into a small space. I do not have a set of printed family trees at home; I rely on printing parts from the computer as I need them. For some people the answer already is to keep the records in a portable computer, and take that to family gatherings and to the record office. Some genealogy packages help the process by having an **indexed book** format, which prints reports as consecutive pages then gives a page index to all the reports at the end. The reports included in this are often **register format**, a narrative ancestor or descendant chart with people numbered according to standards developed in the United States. This style of report has proved convenient for display on Web pages via the Internet; figure 4 in Section 1 is a section of a register format report.

1 Alice Almond b: 9 Jul 1825 in Over Darwen, Lancs src: Wesleyan baptism register
...... 2 James Henry Almond b: 20 Apr 1843 in Lower Darwen, Lancs src: cert (no father named).
   +Henry Slater Bowker b: 5 Jun 1829 in Oswaldtwistle, Lancs src: Date in baptism register, Hippings Wesleyan
...... 2 Mary Hannah Bowker b: 7 Jul 1849 in 5 Howard St, Blackburn src: cert.
...... 2 Joseph Henry Bowker, Rev. b: 9 Apr 1867 in Blackburn, Lancs src: cert.
.... +Harriet Ann Lilburn b: 3 Aug 1874 in Lincoln src: cert.
.... 3 Henry Alan Bowker, MC FCA b: 5 May 1896 src: family
.... +Kathleen Stanhope Lister b: 10 Jul 1898 in Bradford, Yorks src: family
.... 3 Alison Bowker b: 18 Jul 1904 in Macclesfield, Cheshire src: cert.
.... +John Arkas Hawgood, Prof. b: 20 Nov 1905 in Brighton, Sussex src: Family & 'Who's Who'

Figure 18. Indented descendants tree, from Family Tree Maker.

Figure 17 is a family tree of descendants printed from Family Tree Maker, which gives more choice than most packages in layout and fonts used. I chose the style of border, the style of box, the title, and a footnote saying when I prepared the tree. For the title, footnote, and each line of information in the boxes I could choose a separate font; I made the names bigger, the death and marriage dates smaller. To fit on a page of a book I wanted a narrow tree, so I chose a layout in which siblings and their spouses are arranged in a vertical column if it saves space. I could have chosen the more usual layout with everyone of the same generation in one row across.

Figure 18 is an indented descendant chart, one more generation than Figure 17 and of compressed appearance. This also is from Family Tree Maker. To show the effect I have only included the birth date and place and source for each person; when I first printed the chart I had the baptism, marriage, occupation, death and burial for each, with sources.

Figure 19 is a birth brief from my wife's paternal grand-father; he was born in London although his parents were married in Australia, so the family emigrated to Australia, bounced back to England, then went to Australia again. This ancestors chart was printed from Pedigree. The information about each person runs on as a narrative, within its column, and there is no space taken up for missing information.

The ability to scan photographs and include them in printed trees is built into most genealogy packages. You can also have colour slides or colour negatives scanned and stored on a CD-ROM. Either with or without photographs, you may have find that even with the great flexibility of tree format in some genealogy packages you cannot get quite what you want. A solution is to use TreeDraw by SpanSoft, a shareware graphical editor for genealogy; this allows you to put lines and symbols and numbers and text just where you want them.

```
                    ┌─William Henry Excell    ─┬─James Carver Excell
                    │  b.16 May 1831           │  C.30 Jan 1792 St
                    │  Warminster, Wilts       │  Peter the Great,
                    │  d.02 Feb 1912           │  Chichester, Sussex
                    │  Melbourne, AUS          │  d.01 Sep 1845
                    │  m.13 Oct 1860 St        │  Warminster,WIL
                    │  Peters, Easter Hill,    │  m.04 Apr 1824 St
                    │  Melbourne, VIC          │  Denys, Warminster,
                    │                          │  Wilts
                    │                          │
 -Melbourne Frederick  ─┤                       └─Sarah Rogers
  William Excell (Fred) │                          C.24 Aug 1800
  b.25 Jun 1865         │                          Kingswood Wesleyan,
  Lewisham, London d.07 │                          Bristol, Glos d.23
  Nov 1946 Melbourne,   │                          Dec 1871 Avenue rd,
  AUS                    │                          Lewisham
                         │
                    └─Mary Anne Blackmore     ─┬─James Blackmore
                       b.09 Jun 1839           │  b.c.1799 St George,
                       Wraxall Somerset        │  Somerset d.17 Jun
                       d.03 Apr 1906           │  1890 Melbourne, AUS
                       Melbourne, AUS          │  m.01 Dec 1828
                                               │  Wraxall, England
                                               │
                                               └─Mary Ann Howland
                                                  b.1810 Stapleton,
                                                  Glos, England d.25
                                                  Nov 1883 St Kilda,
                                                  Melbourne, Australia
```

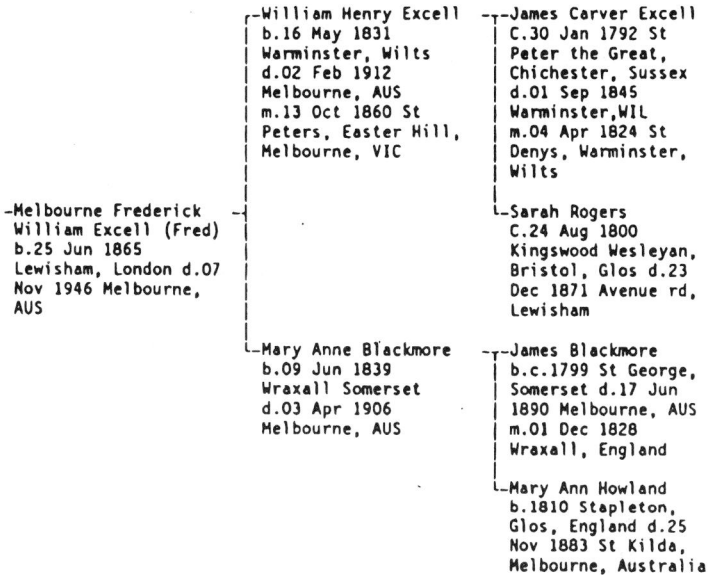

Figure 19. Ancestors Tree (Birth Brief) from Pedigree.

GEDCOM data transfer standard

GEDCOM stands for GEnealogical Data COMmunication. It is a standard developed by the LDS Church to make it possible to transfer information between different computers, and different genealogy systems. The standard defines the format of the file to be transferred. The programs to convert information between the GEDCOM format and the special format of a genealogy package are generally incorporated into the package.

To transfer information between different packages on different computers you run the GEDCOM export program built into the first, take the resultant file to the other computer on a floppy disk or over a communications line, then run the GEDCOM import program in the second package. In some cases that's all there is to it, sometimes you have to modify settings in one package or the other to get the information transferred. If the first package has some fields not available in the second package, you may be able to transfer them to the general notes field in the second package.

GEDCOM is available for transferring IGI and Ancestral File information from LDS Church computers to yours: see next Section. Also, you can send your pedigree as a GEDCOM file to Salt Lake City to be added to Ancestral File or Pedigree Resource File, and be preserved for the future.

Commercial and Shareware Programs and copies from Internet
Some very good genealogy packages can be copied (downloaded) from the Internet and used, completely free of charge — examples are Legacy and Personal Ancestral File. Other programs are marketed in two different ways. The first is a normal **commercial** transaction. You buy a copy of the program from the publisher or a dealer — either by downloading it from the Internet or by buying a disk. You can use it on your own computer, but cannot make a copy for anyone else. Use of a commercial program without paying is piracy. Examples of commercial programs are Family Tree Maker, Family Origins, and Pedigree. The second method is **shareware**. You can legally obtain a copy of a shareware program from a friend, or via the Internet. Alternatively you can pay a shareware supplier to make a copy. But at this stage no money goes to the author or publisher. You can try the program; the manual is a file on the disk with the program, so you can print it. If you decide to continue to use it, you register by sending a fee to the publisher. In return for the registration fee, you usually get a new copy of the program, sometimes a newer version or with extra facilities. The number of shareware programs has reduced, as some suppliers prefer to make a small charge for obtaining a copy of the program, but there are still excellent genealogy programs available as shareware, for example Brother's Keeper, Kith & Kin, and TreeDraw.

See Section 5 for addresses of suppliers of some genealogy packages.

SECTION FOUR

Family Research

This section is about using a computer to produce a list. Typically we start from a source document with events in the lives of people who may be relatives. The computer can help us to select those of interest, sort them into order by name or date or place, then print as a neat table.

Figure 20 is a table of extracts from the General Register Office Index of deaths. There are several ways to produce tables like this. You can use a word processor, spreadsheet, genealogy package or general purpose database. To start with, try using the one with which you are most familiar.

Using Word Processors and Spreadsheets

Originally spreadsheets were for tables of numbers, word processors for continuous text, and databases for lists. But the facilities of the different types of package now merge into each other. To produce Figure 20, I used the word processor WordPerfect; within it I used the Table facility, which is very like a spreadsheet. At first I pressed a function key and asked for a table of 7 rows x 6 columns. This allows two columns for the name, (surname and forenames), so that I could sort or select on either. It also allows two columns for the date, (year and quarter), so that I could do a calculation on the year column. Once I had the basic layout I just typed my information into this.

SAPP. All deaths from GRO Index, Dec 1963 - Jun 1965							
Yr	Qtr	Surname	Forenames	Age	Reg. District & Ref	Born c.	cert.
1963	Dec	Sapp	Harriet M A	64	Kensington 5C 1046	1899	
1964	Mar	- none					
1964	Jun	- none					
1964	Sep	Sapp	Thomas A	63	B. Stortford 4B 24	1901	
1964	Dec	- none					
1965	Mar	- none					
1965	Jun	Sapp	Margaret J	88	Kingston/Thames 5C 761	1877	*

Figure 20. Tables from the General Register Office Deaths Index.

39

I decided to add two heading lines. I also added a column to show the certificates I had applied for, and a column for the calculated year of birth. This last was the only one which used the 'spreadsheet' facilities.

In a spreadsheet each column is given a letter, and each row is given a number. One position in the table is a **cell**. So I moved the highlight to the 'born' column for the first entry; column G and row 3, so it is cell G3. I pressed **M** for Maths, then chose 'formula'. Column A is the year of death (1963), column E is the age at death (64), so I typed the formula A-E. What appeared as if by magic was ... well actually it was not 1899, it was 1,899. Computers never do quite what you want first time. Close enough for the moment, I decided. So I copied the formula down the rest of the column, and changed settings later to tidy up the commas.

The advantage of this approach, using a word processor or spreadsheet, is that it is very easy to get started and get a list printed. As you become more experienced you can make more changes to the appearance and order of the information.

When I first tried the table I entered every quarter for a few years, and as shown just put "none" for quarters with no deaths for the surname Sapp. When I printed the table later I decided not to have a row for a year with no entries, but to have a separate list of sources showing what years I had searched. It is always worth entering some trial data and going through to a publishable result before entering the mass of data.

Data from Internet and CD-ROM

There is now a mass of data available on the Internet or on CDROM. Some of it can be copied directly into genealogy packages using GEDCOM. Others can be copied indirectly, by copy and paste of items of text or by producing a table and converting it into a spreadsheet or database.

As an example consider the IGI and Ancestral File, which were among the first large databases available in electronic form. The LDS Church has them available for search on computers at most of its Family History Centres, and on Internet. The IGI has hundreds of millions of records, mainly baptisms and marriages transcribed systematically from parish registers. The Ancestral File has details of millions of people in linked pedigrees; many now have been sent in by family historians as GEDCOM files from their own computers. In due course, when you have your own linked family records in a genealogy package, you can preserve the information for the future by adding it to Ancestral File. (Also now to the similar Pedigree Resource File).

You can search by name of person, names of parents, area and period for people of interest, then transfer selected records into your computer, via a floppy disk if using the CDROM version. The only charge is the cost of the floppy disk itself. The system, which is called FamilySearch, is easy to use.

When copying records to your disk, you can select either ASCII or GEDCOM format. The ASCII file is ready to print as four lines per event on your computer with a word processor or other printing program. GEDCOM is a special file format which can be transferred into most genealogy packages. If you transfer a baptism from the IGI into a genealogy package, the result is separate records for the child, the father and the mother together with a family record linking them. This has the advantage that, if you search by name in your genealogy package, you get both children and parents of that name. It has the disadvantage that each baptism produces three records, each marriage two records.

There are programs which help in analysing IGI data, transferring it into word processors, spreadsheets and general purpose database packages, and displaying it on maps. For example BIRDIE provides analysis and distribution maps, LDS Companion provides data conversion, GenMap UK provides detailed maps and distribution maps. These programs are available from a number of suppliers: see Section 5.

Because it is so easy to make searches on the Internet it is tempting not to look elsewhere. But only a tiny proportion of genealogy information is available on the Internet. Consider what records you should be searching, then pursue them via the Internet, CDROMs, indexes from family history societies, and visits to libraries and record offices.

Using genealogy packages for lists and research

Most packages have some preset lists available, at least to print names, birth dates and death dates. Using the preset lists is simple, any choices are made from lists of alternatives. Most packages also have **custom reports**, where you can choose which pieces of information to print. On some packages, for example Personal Ancestral File and Pedigree, you can also select which records to print and choose the sort order. The terminology for controlling these starts to assume a knowledge of computer techniques, and to resemble general purpose databases. Genealogy packages have date formats suitable for entering a full date, or partial date, or approximate date; in this respect they are better than spreadsheets and general purpose databases.

You can transfer IGI data in GEDCOM form direct into most genealogy packages. Doing this can add a considerable number of unrelated individuals; it is better to put them in a separate file, away from the file with details of your known linked family.

Some genealogy packages are designed with particular facilities for handling linked and unlinked research information. Pedigree and The Master Genealogist are among them. They may be harder to use initially than some other packages, and may not have such wide flexibility in formatting trees and charts, but score heavily in documenting sources and organising research data. Custodian goes further in specialisation, it provides good research facilities for many different types of data, but does not hold linked family information and does not print family trees.

General Purpose Databases

Database packages are designed for handling lists of information, so they should be suitable for compiling and organising lists of events in family research. But when starting to use computers, databases are not easy to comprehend. They need more computer technique than word processors, genealogy packages and spreadsheets. You will have to be aware of field names, data type, selection criteria, and possibly field length. In any large project it is worth the effort. Once you have information in a well designed database, you can analyse and re-arrange it in ways which are not possible in the other types of package.

Just as word processors have been made as easy as possible to use without specialist knowledge, so databases and spreadsheets have been made easier. If you import a table with headings, some of them will automatically take the column headings as field names, and will analyse the contents of the columns to choose a data type.

Fields and Records

Figure 20 was described in terms of its appearance on paper; a row for each person, a column for each item of information. In computer database terminology each row, i.e. each person, occupies a record; each column, i.e. each item of information, is a field.

When you choose column headings or field names you will start with natural ones: Name, Sex, Date, Place, Event, Document, Relatives, Notes. Depending how you are going to sort and select data, you may decide to split them up. 'Name' naturally splits into Forenames and Surname, maybe you also want Title.

It is always worth having a Notes field. It is tempting to allocate a column for every conceivable type of information that appears in the original record. In parish registers sometimes there is an occupation, sometimes there is a cause of death, sometimes there is a residence. If these only appear occasionally, it is much simpler to put them into the notes field. But do not be tempted to mix types of information, except in the Notes field. For example, I started putting occupations into a Title field, and regretted it later. I have also seen cause of death popped into a Place field. Much better to put them in the Notes field.

The set of fields you use will depend on the original information, but I suggest the following as a start:

Surname	Date
Forenames	Date-Note
Sex	Place
Relatives	Source
Event	Notes

If you use abbreviations, make sure there is a list of them readily available to anyone using the database. I prefer at least three characters as an abbreviation for 'Event'; otherwise there is an immediate problem because Birth and Burial both begin with B.

'Relatives' covers other associates. If they are the obvious ones for the event, I just put their names, e.g. the name of the spouse in a marriage, or the parents at a christening. Otherwise I put the status in brackets. For example recording the apprenticeship of Thomas Hawgood as a farrier in Badby, Northants in 1721 I would put as relatives: John Hawgood (father), Jno & Wm Barnes (master).

For source, I try to give first the natural reference that would enable someone else to find the entry. It is more useful to show a source as 'Parish Register of New Shoreham, Sussex' than to give an accession number or film number. But I keep a separate list of sources with much more detail about where I consulted a document, who transcribed it, and whether I have a photocopy.

Relational Database

In a relational database, two lists are linked by having a field common to both. An example is a register of member's interests in a Family History Society. There is a numbered list of members with names and addresses. The other list shows surnames of interest, with periods and areas, and references to members by their numbers alone. The advantage is that surnames of interest are in alphabetical order, and addresses of members are only printed once. For your own family research, one case where a relational database can help is in holding census records. The address of the household, date, PRO Piece Number, etc can be in one file; names and occupations etc of individuals can be in the other file.

Data from Disks

Some genealogy packages, for example Family Tree Maker, have optional CD-ROM disks with indexes to genealogical sources. These may be family trees submitted by users of the package, they may be indexes to original records. Up to now much of this information has been from the USA, but the scope is spreading. Various substantial indexes are being published on CD-ROM. For example the index to the complete 1881 census for the United Kingdom has been published by the LDS Church. There are various biographical databases, e.g. the Dictionary of National Biography. County archives and Family History Societies are beginning to publish on CD-ROM. Usually a search program is included on the CD-ROM. You just load the disk, the program starts running and gives instructions for making searches.

Internet for family research

At present the Internet is more useful for correspondence and finding background information than for searching indexes to original records. But more indexes are becoming searchable on the World Wide Web. The first use of Internet is email to keep in touch with members of the family and other known friends. Next, you can join email conferences and newsgroups so you can discuss problems and hear news in a group of people with similar interests — for example everyone doing research in a particular county. On the World Wide Web, the best way of finding relatives and people studying the same surname is to publish your own information. Genealogy packages like Family Origins and Family Tree Maker provide web sites where their users can publish their pedigrees, often free of charge. The World Wide Web is very useful if you need background information. It has library catalogues and lists of holdings, for example the Society of Genealogists publishes a list of its parish register copies on the Web. There is information about Family History Societies, archives, general information about places, and much more. See Section 5 for some books about use of the Internet.

Addresses, Bibliography and Help

Computers are still harder to use than any domestic appliances such as video-recorders but millions have mastered them for home use. If you are new to computing try to get help: by attending a local course on word processing; by reading computer magazines; or, best of all, by talking to a computer-literate friend and using their computer.

Family History is a co-operative hobby. If you ask another family historian who uses a computer for advice, you will at least get details of a method they find successful. So approach (and hopefully join) your local Family History Society: find their web page, or send a stamped addressed envelope to the Secretary with a letter asking about members using computers. You can get addresses of Societies by writing (with an sae) to the Federation of Family History Societies, publisher of this book. Some societies have formal computer groups.

Use the Help facilities of your computer – for the operating system and applications. Printed manuals tend to be minimal now, but often there is a printable manual on CDROM and also extensive on-line help available while running a program.

Once you are using the Internet there is even more help available. If you have a question, try putting the significant words into a search engine like Google <www.google.com>. Then try asking the question on an Internet email list – to find a relevant one choose "Frequently Asked Questions" from <www.genuki.org.uk> and follow links from "Is there a mailing list for ????".

Data Protection

The Information Commissioner is responsible for the Data Protection Act, and is at Wycliffe House, Water Lane, Wilmslow, Cheshire SK9 5AF; web <www.dataprotection.gov.uk>, phone (not recommended) 01625 545 745. Data held by an individual and held only for recreational purposes, or data held for management of personal, family or household affairs, are exempt; so most family historians do not need to register.

Magazines

The following magazines contain articles, information about web sites, reviews of genealogy packages and data CDs, and details of user groups for specific packages.

Computers in Genealogy is published quarterly by the Society of Genealogists, 14 Charterhouse Buildings, London EC1M 7BA; web <www.sog.org.uk> phone 020 7702 5483.

Genealogical Computing is a quarterly from MyFamily.com, Inc. Phone (toll free in USA) 1-800-262-3787, web <www.ancestry.lycos.com/learn/publications/gencomp.htm>.

Family Tree Magazine is a monthly, available on news-stands or from ABM Publishing Ltd, 61 Great Whyte, Ramsey, Huntingdon, Cambs, PE26 1HJ; phone (01487) 814050. <www.family-tree.co.uk>. They also publish **Practical Family History** aimed at beginners.

Family History Monthly is published by Diamond Publishing Group Ltd, 45 St Mary's Road, London W5 5RQ, phone 020 8579 1082, email fhm@dpgmags.co.uk.

Ancestors is published bi-monthly by the Public Record Office, Kew, Richmond, Surrey TW9 4DU. <www.pro.gov.uk>

Books

Published jointly by FFHS Publications Ltd and David Hawgood:

David Hawgood, **Family Search on the Internet**, 1999. How to search the IGI, Ancestral File, and other LDS databases.

David Hawgood, **GENUKI — U.K. & Ireland Genealogy on Internet**, 2000. Description and method of use of this major web site.

Published by David Hawgood and distributed by Family Tree Magazine, also available from FFHS:

Peter Christian, **Finding Genealogy on the Internet**, 2nd edn 2002. How to use search engines, gateways, directories, and on-line databases.

David Hawgood, **Internet for Genealogy**, 2nd edn 1999. Introduction to the use of email, newsgroups, mailing lists, the World Wide Web, and various ways of searching for surnames.

Peter Christian, **Web Publishing for Genealogy**, 2nd edn 1999. How to publish your own family history on the World Wide Web.

David Hawgood, **GEDCOM Data Transfer — moving your family tree**, 3rd Edn 1999. Describes the effective transfer standard for moving information between genealogy packages, with examples from Personal Ancestral File and the IGI.

David Hawgood, **IGI on Computer**, 1998. (New edition in preparation). How to search the IGI on CD-ROM, and how to use data from the IGI on your own computer.

David Tippey, **Genealogy on the Macintosh**, 1996. Comparison of genealogy packages for the Apple Macintosh, and use of general purpose software for genealogy. David Tippey writes regularly in *Family History Monthly* (see above) and includes updates on Macintosh software.

Published by FFHS Publications Ltd jointly with S.A. and M.J. Raymond of PO Box 35, Exeter EX1 3YZ, web <www.soft.net.uk/samjraymond/igb.htm>:

Stuart Raymond, **British Family History on CD**, 2001. 128 page book lists available CDs and other data disks.

Stuart Raymond, **Irish Family History on the Web: a Directory**, 2001

Stuart Raymond, **Family History on the Web — an Internet Directory for England and Wales**, 2002/3.

RS Designs, 60 Grasmere, Macclesfield, Cheshire, SK11 8PL, web <www.rs-designs.net> publish guides originally by **Ray Sarfas** (who died in 2001), being continued by his wife Ann Sarfas. Some are available from the Society of Genealogists. Fifteen books include **Beginners Guide to the Internet, Use your Computer to draw better Trees** and **Writing up your Family History with Microsoft Word**.

Peter Christian, **The Genealogist's Internet**, Public Record Office 2001. A comprehensive 208 page book. See "magazines" above for PRO address.

Computer Aided Genealogy, by Nigel Bayley, 2nd edn 1998, published by S & N Genealogy Supplies (address below). Review of packages available, with sections on the use of scanners and photographs. Includes a CD with shareware and demonstration versions

Other books are available — reviews in *Computers in Genealogy* and *Family Tree Magazine* are good sources of information, the bookshops of FFHS Publications, Family Tree Magazine, Society of Genealogists and S & N Genealogy Supplies have a wider selection of books.

Suppliers of genealogy packages, data and books

This list gives suppliers who deal in several products. Suppliers given are in the United Kingdom. Packages available change frequently — it is advisable to read reviews and obtain up-to-date catalogues when purchasing.

FFHS Publications Ltd, Units 15/16, Chesham Industrial centre, Oram St, Bury BL9 6EN, web <www.familyhistorybooks.co.uk>, phone 0161 797 3843. Books, some data CDs (National Burial Index).

Back to Roots Family History Service, 16 Arrowsmith Drive, Stonehouse, Glos GL10 2QR, web <www.backtoroots.co.uk>, freephone 0800 2985984, phone/fax 01453 821300. Many data disks, some genealogy packages.

GenFair at <www.genfair.com> is an on-line family history fair, enabling credit card purchase of books, microfiche and data disks from many family history societies.

PDSL, PO Box 131, Crowborough, Sussex TN6 1WS Tel: 01892 663298, fax 0892 667473, web <www.pdsl.com>. Shareware supplier (but note some products available are old editions).

S & N Genealogy Supplies, West Wing, Manor Farm, Chilmark, Salisbury, Wilts SP3 5AG; Web <www.genealogy.demon.co.uk>, Tel 01722 716121, fax 01722 716160. Dealer in many packages and data disks, also publish census facsimile and other CDs.

Society of Genealogists (address see 'magazines' above). Dealer in many packages, books and CDs.

TWR Computing, Clapstile Farm, Alpheton, Sudbury, Suffolk CO10 9BN, web <www.twrcomputing.co.uk> Tel: 01284 828271. Dealer in many packages and CDs; also sells computers.

Publishers of genealogy packages and utilities

For most publishers only a web address is given. For those not given try Open Directory on the web at <http://dmoz.org>, or use a search engine like <www.google.com>.

BIRDIE from Drake Software, 32 Sixty Acres Road, Prestwood, Bucks, HP16 0PE. <www.drake-software.co.uk>

Brother's Keeper from John Steed. <http://ourworld.compuserve.com/homepages/Brothers_Keeper>

Personal Ancestral File from **Church of Jesus Christ of Latter-day Saints**, free download from <www.familysearch.org> which includes searches of IGI and Ancestral File, also from UK Distribution Centre, 399 Garretts Green Lane, Birmingham, B33 0UH; Tel 0121 785 2200. Also publish data on disk (1881 census, library catalogue, Vital Records Index, etc).

Cumberland Family Tree <www.cf-software.com/cftw.html>

Custodian from P.A. and S. Smith, PO Box 180, Hereford HR4 7YP, Office phone 07801 503144 (mobile), web <www.custodian2.co.uk>. There is a shareware version.

Family Origins <http://formalsoft.com>

Family Tree Maker <http://familytreemaker.genealogy.com>

LDS Companion and **GenMap UK**, Steve Archer, 90 St Albans Road, Dartford, Kent DA1 1TY. <http://ourworld.compuserve.com/homepages/steve_archer>

Legacy Millennia Corporation, Duvall, WA 98019, USA. <www.legacyfamilytree.com>. Free download of complete program.

Pedigree Software, 123 Links Drive, Solihull B91 2DJ, phone 0121 704 2839, <http://ourworld.compuserve.com/homepages/PedigreeSoftware/>

The Master Genealogist <http://www.whollygenes.com>

TreeDraw, Kith & Kin, (shareware) from Spansoft, 8 Juniper Hill, Glenrothes, KY7 5TH, Scotland. Phone/fax 01592 743110. <www.spansoft.org>.

Index